THE DEMENTED CHAUFFEUR
& Other Mysteries

MICHAEL C FORD

Grateful acknowledgment to the following for being hospitable to this book's selected work from both print and online publications.

Ariel • Bakunin • Blank Gun Silencer • Chiron Review
Cultural Echo • Daylight to Midnight • Driver's Side Airbag
Energy West • Gridlock • Kulturleserbrief • Liquid Ohio
Louder Than Bombs • Media Cake Magazine
November Third Club • On Target • Onthebus
Philadelphia Poets • Red Dance Floor
Santa Monica Review • Silver Vein • Speechless
The Moment

Front Cover Photography: Jody Frost
frostfotos.net
Cover Model, Stephanie Battiste
Author photo by Gil Mellé
Cover Design by Rain Livengood

Library of Congress
ISBN 978-0-9817143-2-5

Copyright © Michael C Ford, 2009

First Edition, 2009

Ion Drive Publishing
IonDrivePublishing.com

A Dedication To

JACK SHADOIAN
&
JAMES TATE

2 of the few solving mysteries in Massachusetts

Table of TripTiks

Moving Violations

Taken for a Ride.....1
Vietnam // Peace Casualties.....2
The Sixties.....3
JFK.....4
Corporate Rock Sucks.....6
Mill Creek Canyon Night Watch.....7
Local Anesthetic.....8
Smog.....10
Hollywood Short Story.....11
Credo Detective.....12
A Rhymed Couplet for the
Fall of the Berlin Wall.....12
When City Council Politicians
Teach Us Total Death Lessons.....13
The Long Island Lolita.....14
Sometimes Blue Dahlias Fade to Black.....15
The Black Dahlia.....16
Bringing the War Back Home.....18
The Six.....20
The Asylum Picnic.....21
The Day they Raped and Abandoned
The Los Angeles Times Book Reviews.....22
Witness to the Prostitution.....23
Is This The O.J. Show
Or Just Another Mojo Show.....24
Visitation Rites.....26
Ammunition.....28
Escape Clause.....29
The Demented Chauffeur.....30

Moving Pictures

Show Business.....35
I Wish I Coulda Been
A Humphrey Bogart *Big Shot*.....36
Clara Bow.....37
The Day My Uncle Divorced Gene Tierney.....38
Corkscrew Alley.....39
The Academy.....40
The Retreat.....42
Dive Bomber.....44
Sherlock Holmes and
The Case of the Chaotic Cat.....45
Marie Windsor / 1961.....46
Stolen Bases / 1951.....47
Homily for Jean Harlow.....48
Chicago Homily for Karyn Kupcinet.....50
Gail Russell.....51
A Connecticut Yankee in the King Arthur Motor
Court Just Outside Long Beach, California.....52
Madonna & Prince are Invited
Aboard the Deathstar.....53
Act of Contrition.....54
Silence in a Talking Picture.....56
A Man Mad Enough to Live Among Monsters.....58

When you think of me, think of 2 men—myself and the chauffeur within me.

— Nathaniel West

What is madness but nobility of the soul at odds with circumstance.

— Theodore Roethke

I know that every good and worthwhile thing stands moment by moment on a razor's edge of danger and must be fought-for.

— Constantine Stanislavsky

PROLOGUE

These poetic narratives, however brief or lengthy, do not, at a glance, retain anything remotely close to gentility, redemption or resolution.

They do seem to be excursions into diverse degrees of nameless fears belonging to, even, those who have, over the years, stepped into the shadows.

Most probably, the dual sections of MOVING PICTURES and MOVING VIOLATIONS, will, in many instances, inspire images of malediction, malevolence and collateral evil. either by direct contact or ingrained danger.

It approaches accomplishment just by insinuating, into this volume, the admixture of exchanges between cinematic variation or hopeless images from diurnal tabloid headlines and how they align with an indelible mark left by the very real atmosphere of American criminal mentality: indicative crimes many of which were either un-prosecuted, unpunished or, even undetected.

This is a climate of contamination in a gloomy landscape of insecurity and depression and desperation. Not much sunshine filling the days of these pages; and the nights are jammed with apprehension, suspicion and doubt…no doubt!

— MCF

Moving Violations

Taken For A Ride

What an intolerable set of circumstances,
more or less, setting the scene for a
ginger-hair'd girl hitch-hiking on a side road
just outside Downer, Minnesota.

Several grass transfers will be an alternative
to whatever trips would end in Valley City.

Although this is 2-thousand miles from any
ocean, long waves of soft skin are very slowly
beginning to break on her modified shoreline.

But difficult to interpret, because it can't
respond to any passionate commitment to
verisimilitude.

Then it gets weird, because, as she feigns an
attack of chronic hysteria, the highway forks off
into the circuitry of South Heart, North Dakota.

And the cunning winds of summer
blast the crossroads on her face
like a cruel furnace.

VIETNAM // PEACE CASUALTIES

Date palms were vibrating by the side of the road. The air was ominous with rumbles. We had to hobble back on makeshift crutches, while Napalm fell like chicken ranches in Rock River, Illinois. Midwestern teenagers

brutalized behind their own backs stand, now, in swirling falling bombardments. They are dazzled by a dusty sunset poison: secret *Agent Orange* filtering through gabled warfare windows in our mansion's broken imagination. We

feel it would have been better to return straight standing deserters than experience this kind of desolation. The war left us wanting to put pistol barrels into our mouths, and glue our brains to the plaster. We are shell-shocked sheets

of nervous glass just like splintered fragments of epic Bardic stanzas: yet, without a lyric sense of reflecting anything , except Southeast Asian tourist trade or MIAs loaded on morphine. Delirious we shake in the hanging shards of our

uniforms. Talk may be cheap, but conversation is, at least, affordable art. Now, the only focus victorious for us lies towards opening, again, a door to an unethical suicide room in a place that condones another eccentric, frantic dance of

patriotic wholesale gun-fire delusion. We are moving, now, as we moved before: like slow murderous circus wagons through startled parlors of Phnom Penh. Our journal pages are jammed with pride or pathos: whatever, soon, would

leave us as abandoned as a carwash in the rain.

The Sixties

could you look at it this way? while missiles of the assassin slice through the brains of America. shredded garments hang in closets of cultural politics. none will ever discover themselves (contrary to Southern Fundamentalist opinion) born again. nevertheless, members of the Senate are passing out musty and fat cigars.

JFK

IT'S ALL RIGHT: THIS COOL CUP OF MILKY WAY
STAR-SPILL OVER THE WATCHING GRAVES: THE
PITIFUL DIGGERS WAIT WITH GRIMY EYES: THEY
ARE WAITING OUT OUR OWN SUCCESSFUL SUICIDES
HAPPENING THROUGH EXECUTIVE CONSPIRACY

INCARNATE: OR MAYBE MURDERED BY GOVERNMENT
AGENTS, CIA SHARPSHOOTERS IN A PANEL TRUCK
BACKED UP BY MAFIA CUBAN NATIONALIST HIT-MEN,
ROGUE COPS, TEXAS OIL MILLIONAIRE PERVERTS: A
BUNCH OF INDUSTRIAL MILITARY CORPORATE PSYCHOPATHS

WHO PUT A TIGHT FRAME AROUND SOME LUNATIC FRINGE FBI
SNITCH: THAT CRACKEDPOT HUMAN DUNCECAP CAMPING IN
A BOOK DEPOSITORY WINDOW. IS THIS WHY SO MANY HORSES
WERE SO RECKLESS & INTENSE? WHY SO MUCH CORTEGE BLOOD
AGGRANDIZES OUR ALREADY OBVIOUS AMERICAN STAIN? WHY

WHAT'S LEFT OF THE EARTH SIMPLY ASSUMES THE BODIES OF THE
SLAIN (17 PERIPHERAL WITNESSES BY WARREN COMMISSION MACHETES
WERE CUT DOWN LIKE SUMMER BRANCHES)? IS THERE ANY POSSIBLE
REASON TO LIFE IN A LIFE SO COMPLETELY VOID OF REASON......AS TO
ROT? NO WONDER THERE'S NO WORK: NO WONDER WE ARE FACTOTEMS

OF DESPONDENCE: BUT LIKE GRADE SCHOOL FAILURE, THOUGH
JOBLESS & HOMELESS & DISENFRANCHISED, WE ARE PROMOTED
INTO A 3RD CLASS ABYSS OF SOCIOPATHIC POVERTY, WE HAVE BEEN
CONFINED IN LIBERAL JAILS. DARBY SLICK WAS CORRECT! WE KNOW
WE BELONG TO THE GREAT SOCIETY NOW: BUT EVEN SAN FRANCISCO

ACID BANDS OBJECT. WHY ELSE WOULD JEFFERSON AIRPLANE STAGE A
1980'S REUNION TOUR: A KIND OF WEIRD RETURN TO THE
ALIENATION OF 1960'S CREATIVE OPTIMISM (WHICH SEEMS
IMMINENT ALL OVER AGAIN)? ISN'T IT BRIGHT AS NAPALM IN NAM?
OR IS IT AS DIM AS ANGELDUST BLOWING IN THE HIGH THWARTED

NARCOTIC AIRS? SHOULDN'T IT BE BRIGHT…SOME SORT OF STAR…
GALACTIC LIGHT SPILLING INTO A TINY STREAM, WHERE THE WATER
IS AS CLEAR AS GIN? WE WANT TO HEAR CHUCK HIGGINS PLAY
PACHUCO HOP **(vomp vee dooh! vomp vo doh!)**
WE WANT TO HEAR THE COASTERS DO *SHOPPIN' FOR CLOTHES*

(tha's right, my man, y'gotta git into some fine vines…jus' step on up to that mirror…dig yourself!) WE WANT TO HEAR THE CLOVERS SING:
one mint julep was the cause of it all! OR ANYTHING: BY RUDY TOOMBS! SO
IS IT JUST THAT THIS FUNERAL (GOING ON SINCE 1963 NOVEMBER) HAS
NO END? IS IT THAT THIS LONG SLOW SLIDE INTO THE CELESTIAL

SEWER WAS ALWAYS INEVITABLE? NOW LOOK AT ALL THIS COOL
SPILLING LIGHT: A MOTHER MORNING STAR…OH SHINE
DOWN ON THE CLOVERS SINGING: *hey miss fannie…you sho' look fine…
tell me please will you be mine… hey now!* ALL THAT WONDROUS SPILL &
SPRINKLE TOGETHER JUST LIKE SAINT THERESE

         SHO
          W
          E
          R
          I
          N
          G
             ROSES

CORPORATE ROCK SUCKS

"And you shall drown in entertainment's endless trance...."
— ***Baudelaire***

Morrison was adverse to the gravity of casual verse opposite aqueducts & highways to translated maps that take us for long drives down really deranged roads. Morrison was totally aware of how we are so continuously electronically seduced into some tormented pit of total commercial acquisition: maybe

enough to buy the big ugly condominium, to rev-up the diesel-driven Nazi Hummer, to do drugs, to do disco, to dress middleclass punk. Morrison would warn us against pawning our sacred instruments which used to be tracked around turntables on the holy spontaneous spin of jazz. Morrison fired warning shots about being

too cosmopolitan: doing the life-in-the-fast-lane boogie & never align ourselves beside those who put their bodies on macrobiotic diets, while their souls are starving to death meditating in front of aerobic buddhas. Morrison insisted upon instruction for learning how to disconnect from all those green & intolerable lights burning everyday

on the ego-gratification Christmas tree. You would not catch Morrison's approval of anyone setting themselves up for the MTV geek-of-the-week award. Morrison did, finally, find himself removing the robes of cut-throat military larceny: exchanging them for combat fatigues & joining all of us dog-soldiers who always seemed to be

barking enough evidence to plan the invasion of poetry

what Jim Morrison, given the chance, might have writ down in a 3rd person response to <u>SST Records & Tapes</u> proprietor Greg Ginn

MILL CREEK CANYON NIGHT WATCH

It's another Wasatch mountain lookout.
Look-out! Misty swirls whiskbrooming what's
seen in the ravine: low trees folding and

unfolding their shroudy arms, like priests
turning water into mirrors of wine. There's
this canyon's luminous green of draining

Ponderosa clusters, these croaking forests, this
mutter of insects, the crunch of a cloistered fawn.
All of it being true counts for summing-up dribbly

clouds mugging the month of my 37th summer. That
rat-a-tat-tatting machine-gun rain against our
lodging. It is marked by a place of no mistakes. There

are no needs for sanction nor forgiveness. Children
camouflaged in a cabin like kidnap victims the
surly inspector has tracked, here. It's a scene

where fog dissolves, where the sun is spilling its morbid light,
and where I've heard so often, even the geese
won't bring anything back.

LOCAL ANESTHETIC

Outward to the place where my little girl cousins lived
In a place no longer lovely; where their brother drove
Abused ambulances, listening to the moans of the
Injured and the insane: siren intrusions boycotting the
Supermarket of night

The Zen-sound crash of a clapping memory of oranges
Was falling like Hiroshima, and I saw the same evil
Madness that buries the China-white oblivescence of
Monterey Park

What can we do about the oppression alienation and
Brainwash they call college? What can we do about
The computerized, fundamentalist television hustle for
Real estate they call religion? I want to see a suburban
Jesus resurrect and spit splinters of the cross into the
Hype and chisel of landlord greed

I want to inspire a cultural revolution and tumble down every
Vast asphalt strip: every ugly sprawling shopping mall Hell:
Every overpriced tract apartment and condo complex
Menacing the landscape

I want to mobilize all of their tenants and do a commando
Raid on the sinister and slimy city councils who make the
Dirty deals

If I'm aware, however, of any other kinds of thug-threat
From whatever else will offend or lacerate their natural
Hearts, I'll have to dynamite these demonic monsters of
Industry and continue my role as word hurler: tossing my
Knuckleball talk into the ears of enemy corporations
Who, without contradiction, continue manipulating and
Pulling strings attached to puppet politicians

They have been so far safe in running bloody numbers: for
Has not the child that dwells, still somehow within what's
Left, been named a strange and secret Moses? He's, as it
Happened once before, concealed within these trembling
Euphrates reeds

So try, just try burning me with effigies of fiery crosses, you
Anti-Christ-crypto-Nazi perverts: the white heat of your hate,
Your KKK artillery ain't no good, because I, alone, know
What precious avenues to use for my getaway: I, alone,
am available to the artful dodge

SMOG

because
the ink in my journal is as
blue as the ocean
because
the sea always seemed
to be the sky
because we witnessed
with wonderful
sewing machine eyes
because
it was always the warp & woof
of summer's bent fabric
because
we were scattered like a
Laguna Beach family of
frantic gulls flapping off into
the birdy air
because
we maintain hope that none
of my mother's nieces
would ever be submerged
in that cancerous industrial
middleclass mindless poison
relentlessly sleeping with them
because
it lies against the stale gray bed
of the San Bernardino Mts.

HOLLYWOOD SHORT STORY

They make a million dollars a year singing American pop trash. They used to hang in some canyon hillside mansion, whereof, in the vicinity, eleven entertainment luminaries, were, through mistaken identity, murdered. Now, they drive around town in Rolls Royce Silver Shadows, Lamborghini Diablos, Mercedes, Maseratis, Renault Five Turbo Ones, Jaguar Two-K-Eights or Beamers: always under the protective *beam* of bodyguards.

And, every once in a while, they find themselves thinking about how very uncomplicated the life of a Puerto Rican busboy must be.

CREDO DETECTIVE

We don't believe
God is dead!

But we really do wish
That somebody would

Put out a missing
Persons report on him.

A RHYMED COUPLET FOR THE FALL OF THE BERLIN WALL

**Edited PRAVDA gangsters
  behind Bolshevist bars
USA TODAY ink like lice
  in the beards of Czars**

WHEN CITY COUNCIL POLITICIANS TEACH US TOTAL DEATH LESSONS

For Katie Ford

I am mad with travel over
rivers and oceans and terribly
enamored with journeys which
all too willfully stumble into the
water, wade, then, jump, dipping
into cinema intonations that are
epitomized by a John Cheever
short story: victims depicted by
Janis Rule and Burt Lancaster
getting cold feet in *The Swimmer*

But down there, where many have
drowned on another coast, where
city government greed-heads will
refuse to pick up a bill insuring
safeguard in favor of the city of
old New Orleans, so privatized
city council parasites who should
be brought up on multiple charges of
aggravated manslaughter could line
their pockets with gold

I am obsessed with Atlantic seaboard
accumulations: soft evidence of mud
and blood gritty as funerals of trust
in a safe house in Baton Rouge. And I
discover we are better off without an
intervention, even, without anything
which doesn't, already, exist in a
Washington DC of Federal corruption.

THE LONG ISLAND LOLITA

you might have sd: *light of my life,*
fire of my loins had you looked a bit more
like James Mason, Joey: maybe, better that than
yet another suburban flame
blazing out of control.

so, you felt sad for her, in a sorry psycho
conflicted sort of way. and what went wrong
with daddy that saw Amy wagging her finger
at a greasemonkey who had all the moral
barometer of a pedophile.

oh, sure, you were hypnotized by her turn-on
teenage mouth, where doves were dive-bombing
the wharf and washing away all your Catholic guilt;
where Flushing, Long Island was hotter than
pinning a very video porno pinup girl up against
the machine shop wall.

the mesmerizing click of her heels was like
pebbles tossed down a chill well. she/ll tell
you she is not Lilith: will not spend 6,000
years with you in fidelity, loyalty and love.
however, you must admit, it did allow you
to follow her into the anteroom of Hell: but
you knew the drill, Joey.

to let her stay any longer than it takes to burn
anything more than the morning coffee
would have been a big mistake.

Sometimes Blue Dahlias
   Fade To Black

This is what I wrote concerning an LA murder mystery: the strange and gruesome death of a woman popularized by the news media as The Back Dahlia.

When I was going to Audubon Jr. Hi, in the mid-1950s, I/d walk 39th Street, over to Santa Barbara Avenue (which was renamed MLK Bv.) in a neighborhood which is now considered part of South Central. Every morn I/d pass the corner at Norton and look at the vacant lot (in process, by then, of groundbreaking for the building of tract houses) and I/d say "That/s where they planted the Dahlia!" It was only about 9 years after the fact, but remember being obsessed with this unsolved homicide, so wanting to write something, sometime, finally, got around to it about 10 years ago. It was published in the summer 2000 issue of a Midwestern literary tabloid: Chiron Review. And I suppose if I/d waited for the movie about her to write this, it could be one of my series of takes on Noir motion pictures or Neo-Noir film. But I ended up beating the timeline by six years; even before The Dahlia Avenger.

The Black Dahlia

Her name was Elizabeth Short and, although only contained 3 letters in the original Hollywood sign, she wanted to be a hot movie starlet. Yet, she settled for being a cold out-call honey-party-girl-tease: rumored to

have been running numbers, servicing, then monitoring aspects of the LA Mob. One cool, overcast weekday morning in 1947, her meticulously tortured and severed body was discovered in a vacant lot on the corner of 39th

& Norton by a Baldwin Hills newspaper delivery boy. Now, anything classified as unsolved, during a time when LAPD had been under heavy scrutiny for egregious corruption, usually implied police were allegedly involved, and a savage killing like

this might reasonably inspire a massive cover-up. What follows will be these endless investigations, rationalized interrogations and, dimly-lit (if not, entirely, black) blind alleys of speculation. At that time, victims of any minority description or,

even, suspected prostitutes, cops tended to describe as NHI: *no humans involved.* Just about 5 days before the Dahlia file had been defoliated (yet not "officially closed") local fuzz were busy with a series of set-ups beginning in the late 1940s and referred to as the

Zoot Suit Riots. **All the while, at various crime scenes, LA Times photojournalists were seen (Weegie-style) lensing the dead and the dying. At the corner of North Alameda & Brooklyn Avenue, Poncho Jesus Perez was bleeding to death: his Brilliantined Indian hair hanging**

in the gutter. One of his blue sharkskin arms was slung, like a crippled hawk's wing into a storm drain. Before he was stuffed into a paddy-wagon bodybag, some sneaky clip-artist severed his gold watch chain at the stem: NO HUMANS INVOLVED! *

* *NHI. So, if you think it/s vicious today, you should have been in trouble circa 1949. Police could be bad white men doing very bad things to people who were not white: cops on the take, undisclosed agendas, rubberhose interrogations.*

How many Hispanics, alone, were forced into confessing to crimes they didn/t commit and ended-up in prison or on death row?

Until the time William H. Parker {a cop who really knew where all the bodies were buried} became Chief, revamping the LAPD all thru the 1950s, undeniable cronyism and prejudice had been rampant. You can imagine the worship Jack Webb received for his Dragnet *radio program (later evolving into TV).* Dragnet *was a very expensive on-going commercial for the new LA Police Dept.*

BRINGING THE WAR BACK HOME

Remembering when the U.S. President:
George, the senior Bush, got food-poisoned
in Japan and hurling all over the Nipponese
flag: in retrospect, a perfect metaphor,
perhaps, for the degenerate perpetration
of *Operation Desert Storm.*

The 1980s were going away and I was
catching a green light, walking across
the terminal illness of Pico Bv. then,
over to my neighborhood street, hoofing
down the driveway, passed the main house
to a used-to-be pool shed dressing room
attached to the former '40s bungalow
residence, there, where I'd been living
for the past 19 years.

the refugee woman from Central America
who escaped being skewered by
CIA-sanctioned fascist police in Nicaragua
was cacked-out in a garden chair
in front of her apartment compartment
adjacent to mine.

She's always been rather decent and friendly and is now holding up this morning's edition of the *Los Angeles Times*: pointing at one of the sub-headlines reporting what the Bush-man did on a visit to Japan.

"Your president is sick," she said.
I answered: "They're the only kinds
who get elected!"

I stepped into my room, took a vintage water pistol off its easel and thought about my father's brother who came back from World War II, moved to Utica, New York, using a similar toy, held up a liquor store for two bottles of *Jameson's* Irish was, immediately apprehended and sentenced to doing a nickel for armed robbery.

Yes! that's the way this country treats its brave and damaged veterans of foreign conflict: so, thinking about all of it, putting the barrel of the water gun against my right temple, nudging the trigger and washing-out my version of Vincent Van Gogh's other ear.

THE SIX

> *Violence Is the result of a loss of
> identity: the greater the loss, the
> the greater the violence*
> *— McLuhan*

In the concrete New York City farmyards
½ dozen eggs broken by some chicken bomb.
If the United States is so vulnerable to sabotage,
then where was the secret service blueprint for

prevention from, yet another slaughter of the
innocents. If to the demented Jihad Egyptian
terror network, an arrogance of monolithic
American architecture is an offense, then why

didn't somebody consider National defense? One
can not put twin tower false gods of monopoly &
greed {or whatever other existing imagined
grievances} 220 stories into the air, then wait for a

conspiracy of brainwashed hit-men to truck-bomb the
basement. After, with a conspicuous lack of purpose,
our *Prez* really "forgot" to empower those agencies,
which would insist upon a rational national safeguard,

in order to amplify protection against allowance of any
future militant extremist assault, all that World Trade
Center symbiosis seems to say: *we dare you to blow it up!*
Well, guess what! Possibly, the dead were not cause for

concern. Tell the families of those six victims that they
were expendable. Maybe, the next diabolical attack on
our soil will leave 600 detonated components of complacent
political International *Nintendo*.

Stockton {1993

THE ASYLUM PICNIC

> *The would-be assassin met his fiancee in a facility for the criminally insane.*
> — *People Magazine* (**1986**)

He continues to superstition several fantasies the radio announcing his past transgression beleaguers. He wants to send *stelazine* messages to the secret police. Even an infernal

ineluctability of Presidential filing cabinets cools off. There's this winsome tyranny of electroshock between a maligned set of bodyguards and Jody Foster we wanted to discuss. As

hostile, as *Taxi Driver* pathological, without the Mohawk, but hot for Jody, as he appeared to be, he tried to pop Reagan. He has had handed back to him enough broken mirrors to inspire

the bad luck of a possible 7 wedding anniversaries. A maniacal ego is thrown, like a stale bridal bouquet from the back of an observation platform on a mansion train painted into one of

those urban art projects on the wall of a *bait and switch* loan company congested with purloined securities. Maximum security jail keeps lessening like the *Flatwheel Limited* going

over a few guilty bridges. And as Jody matures into some rape victim, on screen, or haunted FBI agent, then does desire die on the hustling wings of imagination's pigeon? And does it

want to fly-off gravestone statuary; what voyeurs visiting cemeteries which resemble so many *Disneylands* for the dead, came to know and love as *doves at dawn*?

THE DAY THEY RAPED AND ABANDONED THE LOS ANGELES TIMES BOOK REVIEWS

And this is the way it happens, when myopic managers of
Major metropolitan newspapers {with usual mindless
Purpose} extinguish the firebrand perceptions inherent
In, maybe, one of the last warriors of Political Journalism.

Then, in the same move, these creatively crippled
Publishers appoint and elevate some literary pimps from
Out of the university brothels to a premiere position, as
Arts editors or book editors, thereby encouraging these
Unsavory self-motivated media censors to ignore
American writers who refuse to play the kiss-poo-suck
Games of vanity editing.

Because of the major mission to invent a new set of cogs
And wheels and toggle-switches inserted into an insane
Global Economic Greed Machine, it is possible for those
Who are chosen culture vultures of the new order to,
Out of excellent foppery, going out of their way to promote
Only the sophisticated swine whose books are puked out
Of the vortex of East Coast Publishing cesspools,
Have allowed the rest of us to be left bereft.

Let me bottom-line you: sometimes, it is necessary to be
Arrogantly preachy in order to reveal the truth.

These kinds of "editors" are evil and dangerous; and any
Tabloid publisher putting them in charge of music or arts or
Books is like putting Adolph Hitler in charge of the Gas Co.

Witness For The Prostitution

{an Irish quatrain for F. Lee Bailey}

Are psychodrama children tried

As jurors want to slay the judge?

TV interprets knives that lied

And witnesses are morphing into sludge!

The following narrative first saw light when actor Cyril O'Reilly verbally dramatized it for the O.J. Follies: *a 1994 program of political sketches produced by Susan R. Rogers, staged at Luna Park in West Hollywood.*

IS THIS THE O.J. SHOW OR JUST ANOTHER MOJO SHOW

Surely, it's a set-up for media greed mongers to get greased by a blitz of lies, gossip, fabrication, innuendo

Now, the nation was in more sinister division than it was, during 12 years of slaughter in Viet Nam

There's been no *reel* celebrity high-roller murder defendant more visible in Hollywood history, since Roscoe "Fatty" Arbuckle, allegedly, raped Virginia Rappe: *The Sunbonnet Girl* and, in the process, killed her with a violently inserted *Coca-Cola* bottle in 1921

So, then, 70 years later, this iconic sports hero (after proving to America just how much it *hurts* to rent a car) after police interrogation for nine previous incidents of spousal battering; and after becoming a reticent candidate for felony homicide conviction, this former football grunt gets a *batterie* of deal-maker lawyers wearing $2,000 *Armani* suits in order to more formally, with an aire of cynical sophistication, contaminate the criminal justice system: traveling by chauffeur-driven limos through the punished streets of racist paranoia

All this tax-payer monopoly game "do not pass go" "go to jail" with arguments of: *no weapon, no witnesses, no case*

I could have done that for him wearing bib-overalls
and drive myself to the goddamn courthouse in a
Chevy flat bed.

NO NO NO! The whole bad bit is that, if, somehow,
this had happened to some cat living on welfare checks
in South Central, he would have been lynched from a
lamp post on the corner of Florence & Normandy

Because, in the scheme of things, in the *scam* of things,
how could a tackling dummy who, once upon a time,
carried a football the length of a gridiron in 9 point 5
possibly be guilty of anything? Yes, I am proud to live in
a country where pig skin is more favored, more honored,
more adored, more idolized than the human skin of a
slaughtered daughter or a decimated son.

And the fool even left a blood trail Angela Lansbury
could have followed, solving the case 57 minutes after the
1st commercial.

Now, the nation may survey the exhibition of bloodsucker
hustlers: an exhibition of one media vampire after another
who just happened to be with neither the brains nor intrinsic
imaginations to compose words which would, maybe, contribute
something sacred to the world culture.

Instead, they're contracting half-million dollar book deals; and the
same no talent, no load, sandbagging barracudas are feeding off
American tabloid television treated sewage: and all because of it
all, there's this exhibition for the standard creeps, the socio-
pathological voyeuristic keyhole peepers who never stop paying
such solicitous attention to artistically arranged trash, we can still
see it hanging upside-down inside media museums of the damned.

VISITATION RITES

There's the feeling Los Angeles should be
a legacy of palmtrees bordering avenues
named after unknown Indian explorers.
But, inside, it's just a place where
you can get channel 5

Mid-1960s new county jail is jam'd with
Saturday visitors: rheumy-eyed and dis-
possessed. There's this working-class girl
six months blimp'd with new baby
complication calling on her old man who
boosted a liquor store in Compton
following too many days of slavery at
Northrop

Everybody looking at one another
through brave tears, through cool sheets
of inconsiderate glass: sometimes, right
through each other. And somebody says:
"Jeeze, honey, I miss you so gosh darn
much"

There's the UCLA film student: Jose Louis Gonzales accused of stabbing his girl friend to death, using 2 kitchen knives with 7-inch blades, in order to, allegedly, liberate the soul of his dead mother. Now, he tells his attorney that he didn't know what he was doing

When you go outside, you look up at those fine green palmtree cutlasses. They seem to *pirate* a tablet of uncommonly clear pure buried treasures of air. So, you know, tomorrow, half the LA population will be offering adoration to a kaleidoscope Christ disguised as a test pattern on Channel 5. And, because of Mount Wilson, you will be able to see it
real plain

AMMUNITION

AFTER Henry Rollins

I got a weapon: it's really
My perception

I know who's free & I know
Who's a slave & I'm waiting for
The world to admit it's insane

I know what I know can sound
Hyper: because I can't let you
Know what I know, unless I see
What I say on my typer

I know who's free & I know
Who's a slave & I'm waiting for
The world to remember its name

I know what movies are made by
Demons on binges: I know what
Music swings on hideous hinges

I know women who wade through
A poet's blood wearing high-style
Gucci galoshes

I know the media pimps who crucify
Modern prophets on their pre-fab,
High-tech, greed-head Golgothas

I know who's free & I know
Who's a slave & I'm waiting for
The world to go up in flames

ESCAPE CLAUSE

Noon! Into the oblivion of sun in Culiacan. Navajoa brings down the warmed-over daylight. Guaymas goes damp as the Gulf mosquitoes of Topolabompo. Lunar moths in Los Mochis, with evanescent insect grace, sail suicidal into the indomitable face of the truck. Nogales crossover / 5:AM. The windshield glass is a translucent bug cemetery. Despite our dirty carriage of death, we show-up clean for the border police.

THE DEMENTED CHAUFFEUR

Je sais l'avenir par coeur
— Valery

Like a bad conduct medal, a busy highway
is hung on this brute country. It's populated
by women whose lacerated hearts, like broken
roadhouse windows, are shot with splinters
of glass: whose eyes glaze over, then crumble

in a way that resembles the fuliginous collapse
of decadent empires. Possibly, if there isn't
anymore than that to be learned from all this, it
would be worth bringing to someone's attention.
Pertinent names of persons or places will, as a

matter of caution, be changed, in order to
prevent the usual onset of hazardous
coincidence, however vague. See, I'm talking
about the time you worked for the estranged
father of a girl who went to school with me at

Aaron Burr Elementary. Her father's name
was Reddy; and he rode in the back seat of this
long black car, but you couldn't tell, until he
got out, because of the tinted windows. They
must have called him Reddy in honor of his

hair which was bristled and the color of orange paint. He owned a roadhouse directly opposite a set of retirement condos known as *God's Waiting Room Village*. It boasted a miniature golf course on one side and a very easily

accommodating cemetery on the other. Once, I remember you said that Reddy, sometimes, let you drive him around in the car with the tinted glass, mainly, because you were his most trusted bartender. I, also, remember you, simply, one day

vanished, turning into an exurban ghost. You just disappeared in *Droopy Willows* with your wife who always reminded me of the girls I loved to look at standing in front of the Snowlight Lounge, or the ones who posed on covers of downtown magazine

racks: the ones with titles like *Model Prisoner*. I don't think I saw you, before you were both, so suddenly, gone. But, if rumors of your, apparently, acrimonious rage were only partially accurate, you must have been burning in a way similar to summer afternoons at

Stinking Desert Dry Lake. I never, totally, understood the necessity of quick departures, until I was old enough to run away myself from whatever began to resemble confusion and abuse. I mean, sometimes, so much happens that a seven year-old isn't supposed to

immediately comprehend. So, then, about 20 years later, during a return nostalgia trip to *Two-way Mirror City*, I make a point of stopping at that roadhouse, walk over to a guy working the bar (it wasn't you anymore, of course) and, when I ask him to what part of the world

you re-located, he pretends, distractedly, to check gimlet glasses for spots. And, when I ask him about Reddy, he points towards the cemetery obliquely, informing me that the former owner had moved across the street about twelve years ago. I guess

you already knew your wife, coincidentally, had the same name as Reddy's daughter. Wasn't it *Sweden*? Or was it *Torchy*? And wasn't she the one they always said would grow up to be associated with images of indolent elegance: then, finally, abandoned

in a glamorous seascape escape; only to return, absolutely, comparable to a type of woman people often used to see in movies about money, limousines and power: a lady who knows how to drive through all that danger?

Moving Pictures

SHOW BUSINESS

It was one of those formica jungle chain diners. All I had in front of me was a glass of tap water containing chemicals with ice-cubes made from tap water full of chemicals. I couldn't help overhearing the next table's conversation: male & female: both lawyers & they

were loud. The woman suggested that the man use her interior decorator, whenever he decided to overhaul his penthouse livingroom. Her decorator would only charge him 250 thousand as opposed to the 300 thousand his had been recommending. The

man, then, began his soliloquy of information: "But my interior decorator's also a singer, a dancer & an actor & one night he invited me to his little theatre group & they were about to start rehearsals for a musical version of IN COLD BLOOD. But that

night they were practicing what's called the art of improvisation & as a joke had me go up on stage & play the part of a prosecuting attorney & that's when it suddenly hit me. Wow, this is the first fun I've had as a lawyer. I say to myself: hey, these actors have

a really good time: I'm thinking, if I become an actor, I can have fun forever. So, that's why I decided on this career switch. Look at all the show business connections I'm already hooked-up with. Why hell, I can be an actor in the movies

without a bit of struggle & have all the fun I want to have from now on." He sounded like every other dilettante artist in America who never needed fine-tuned sensibilities, talent or desire. His voice sounded weak, dull, witless, mediocre, secure, safe & boring. He will be a major star.

I WISH I COULDA BEEN A HUMPHREY BOGART
BIG SHOT
After Monica Gayle

That is I coulda been a Humphrey Bogart
Big shot with Irene Manning mixing
Betty Crocker batter in a bowl by blaze
Of hearth in a mountain cabin hideout.

Oh, 1942, I coulda turned blue with lust,
With love! I dunno……whatever! Irene,
Irene, our luck ran out on stool-pigeon feet.

Where did you go? Now in a time, when
I must be slow as the rest, where are your
Furs or expensive print dress? Your fine
Stiletto-heels mark my escape in the snow
Covering yesterday's dust of capitulation.

But, I still gotta know: why did you go,
Leaving us alone with 1990's starlets wearing flat
Serbian sandals of no particular sex

If this were translated into saloon singer persona, it would be my torchy ballad. It was composed after viewing the 1932 movie, **Call Her Savage,** *during 1970s music tour, in my hotel lobby television midnight cool down insomnia. I ask this old jazzer who she was. He answers: "Well, son, mostly some kind of silent screen star and she was buried about 10 years ago in a graveyard about 3 miles from Culver City."*

CLARA BOW

> *They are all gone, now; the days we thought would never come for us are here.*
> — **Kenneth Rexroth**

Clara Bow   you never knew I know
May never know   how now I see you
Like in a dream   last night tells me
You were as you   were on late late
Show TV   when they called you
Savage inside   19th Century epic
West   how your troubles
Compounded with   tears   how you
Began to mean   more to me than
My own life   how I wanted to
Tell you   this now it's too   late
Somebody said tonight   the way you
Died alone   in Culver City   in 1965
No   it can't be too   late I know
You're still   alive   I'll be able to
See you   touch you kiss   your
Spangled hair   drive   your car
Backwards   to a compatible
Year   all this although   I know
Everything is   still okay   know you
Are only a few miles   away because
I believe what I   see in the movies

THE DAY MY UNCLE DIVORCED GENE TIERNEY

I mean that's the way it was it seemed because
I started going to movies at the age of three it
Was better than babysitters or so my parents

Decided and it wasn't too surprising when I
Began to indemnify unreasonable realities
With a whole lot of infantile identifications

And when I looked at my uncle's 2nd wife for
The last time through a window on the *Illinois
Central* she was like a 1945 *Laura* portrait blue

Hat with fishnet veil and how she'd blink back
Tears on the night train and how I waved kind
Of flexing my fingers…... unsteady as triggers.

*This was the original title for the Eagle-Lion film **Raw Deal**, which, if it were not for the hard-edged directorial eye of Anthony Mann, might have easily been just another routine chase movie: rather than the dizzying, moody, thoroughly enthralling thriller classic it turned out to be.*

CORKSCREW ALLEY

**It seems as though forever, since you,
from that memorial balcony, were beckoning
by your silent call. Your burning consolation
in darkness, was that *Raymond Theatre*
reincarnation: *Crown Theatre*, Pasadena**

**1949. Yes, you'd seen us, there: cinema's
gray grammar-school phantoms. And the
way we idealized your precious name:
Marsha Hunt. You were too young to be
our mother, exactly: you were sister to our**

**cinematic spirits: brave, pretty perfect,
protective, smart, compassionate, comforting,
crying because we were dying: more than ever
pretending to be Dennis O'Keefe avenging raw
deals everywhere. Soon, Claire Trevor's tears**

**commingled with yours and our imaginary
blood boils all over an *RKO Radio Picture*
sound stage imitation of a remote
San Francisco sidewalk.**

THE ACADEMY

> *The local is the only universal;*
> *upon that all art builds*
> *— John Dewey*

Like a story that recalls a fable
About time eroding rural
Landscape occurrences,
American architecture
                        Crumples

Inside the "fist of progress"
Mentality. For example,
Here's another fugitive town: Pasadena,
Californy. There, just before
Colorado Boulevard

                        Dwindles
Into Arcadia, it was nice to see this
Forbearance of metal up above the
Academy cinema rooftop: contradicting
Bravely the more fearful installations.

                        This
Was a miniature radio cable derrick: inverted
Cone-shaped erectorset-like lattice-work with
Spiky sphere on dome-point, upwardly as
Sputnik or a motionless ballroom strobe:

Ironically round as the wrecking ball of
Urban renewal. Surely, it was unattractive,
Yet remarkable: just like an elephant
On waterskis. Then, in that same sputtery way
An importance of steamboats

                              Disappeared.
Eventually transforming travel into just one
More crude negation of mileage, this vacant
Roof turns deserted as a war-cracked
French cathedral. Of course, there is an

Argument, also, in the sense that some
Reminiscence has its methods of audacity:
But lots of emporiums, at one time, being
Hospitable to us, are gone as Edsels: The Park
The Oaks The Pasadena The Tower The Strand

The Raymond the Ritz the Uptown the
Crown: only a stagger of storefronts
Or of variously abused alterations, now.
                              However
In order to preclude any cynical intrusion

It should be noted that all this woozy
Nostalgia isn't to suggest we are not entirely
Void of certain necessary realities. We have
                         For example
An innate ability to retain paean choruses from

Cole Porter lyrics, as well as saccharine elements
associated with a coterie of
Warner Bros. bit players,
                         Yes!
We are, surprisingly, at the same moment,

Capable of remembering that
Moline, Illinois
Has always been celebrated as
The farm equipment
Capitol of the world.

THE RETREAT

Wishing to deny attitudes of
Impatience & dissatisfaction,
I decide to move to the planet
Mars

The weekend I arrive crystalline
Kids throw stolen plutonium stones
At glass houses every night

During the day, with hands marked
By a leprosy of spiders, they applaud
Themselves through truant alleyways

There is treachery in every tree they
Climb: it's a question now of how much
Hostility I can stand in one sitting

I lock my door from the inside of a Galaxy 6
Motel, then boost myself over the sill of a
Chink'd window

Winter blisters in my hair: pink moonlight
Wobbles on a shrinking canal

I swim across to the other shore side: what's
left of my identity becomes debris that mixes
With drainage underwater: my senses turn
Into anthropological ghost stories: my star
Eyes go Cro-Magnon: it isn't long before
Scrawny lavender branches begin to umbrella
My primitive head

I'm armed only with sticks & a butane lighter
From the Jupiter Boutique on Europa: I
Build a fire: I crouch & dream with other
Disillusioned tourists

Suddenly, we're surrounded by radar cars,
Placed in plastic cages, then paraded through
The narrow streets of transparent towns

It doesn't take any time at all to admit to the
Truth of a well-entrenched Martian aphorism:
"the grass is always redder on the other side
of the senses"

DIVE BOMBER

During WW2, my father's brother, as a member of the US Air Force was shot down 3 times over Germany, forced to bail out, miraculously making his way back through the Bundt underground: and in order to take his conscious mind as far away from the dangers of enemy ack-ack torching his chute and turning him into a Roman candle, he'd imagine himself in one of those H. Rider Haggard- type 1930's pulp adventure fantasies.

It was a 1944 of hostiles: high priestess trailing her silken gown over the sexes of lost pilots They're imprisoned in the new dungeon: all the rest parachuted into the steaming jungle

"You can not leave here, now," she sd. Cut diamonds shaped like ball turrets roll across the cobbled floor of the fortress

"You can not leave, now!" She walks with you like an anxiety of speculative fiction. There's the linking of arms under the smoking trees. She's the boss: she's in love with you. "You can not leave, now!"

The others before you have been tortured for years. Young branches whip the stars. A split-second jailbreak brings the war right back down to earth

You're the last one to recognize the reality of where you are.
"Hey, you!"
"Me?!
"Yes, you: you can not leave now!"
"Why not?"
"We just might want to murder someone!"

SHERLOCK HOLMES AND THE CASE OF THE CHAOTIC CAT

(To be read with an accent in the Sir Arthur Conan Doyle tradition)

    BLAST IT, HOLMES, PUT DOWN THAT VIAL OF LIQUID COCAINE AND LISTEN TO MY SOMEWHAT EGREGIOUS, ALBEIT ENLIGHTENED, ACCOUNT OF A CAT WHO , IN ALL INELUCTABILITY, HAS BEEN SO NAMED CHAOS! THIS FELINE EXHIBITIONIST, NOT ONLY DOES THESE IMITATIONS OF TV CAT FOOD COMMERCIALS, BUT (I DO SOLEMNLY FORESWEAR) MORPHS INTO A BLOODY AWFUL PANTHER POUNCING TO THE ROOFBEAMS AND PRANCING, I DARESAY, HE STRADDLES AND STROLLS THE NETWORK OF WOODEN STRUTS LIKE A FORTRESS GUARD.

    HOWEVER, WITHIN THE WALLS OF THIS CROOKS CASTLE, THIS DRAKE DOMICILE, THIS VERITIBLE HOUSE OF JUSTICE, IF I MAY BE SO BOLD AS TO SAY, DUE TO THE IRONIC TRESPASS OF THIS CHAOTIC CAT, ALL OUR HOPES (THOUGH THEY DO SEEM TO BE, AT TIMES, DASHED FOREVER IN TERRIBLY TERRIBLY HOPELESS DISARRAY) ARE SUDDENLY MIRACULOUSLY RAISED AS THE VERY ROOFBEAMS THEMSELVES ON HIGH, WHICH REMINDS ME, HOLMES, YOU BLOODY BASTARD, YOU MAY NOW RETURN TO THE NEEDS TANTEMOUNT TO YOUR OWN ELEMENTARY ELEVATION .

MARIE WINDSOR / 1961

Remembering her, always,
as the quintessential brunette
femme fatale: even, in her
crossover to 1960s television
when she, still, in series reruns
moves across the silver screen
like 125 pounds of warm fog.

She always essayed the kind
of woman who was this
troublemaker on *The Untouchables*,
or a perpetrator on *The Rifleman*
or murder victim on *Perry Mason*.

A woman, then, who kept reinventing
herself, as a counterpoint of feminine
infinites: even with special consideration
directed towards Belle Starr lady outlaw
buckskin barometer, through decrepit
rooms reinforcing evil, or in a bad place
of narrow margins, where the sniper
draws his envious bead. The sultry sound
her lush voice makes is velvet
stretched across a field of gravel.

Always, it would seem to be some sort
of scene, where all these television
heavies: all those gray guys (good or
bad) got stoned.

STOLEN BASES / 1951

Dickie say: put the tunnel over there   the
vacant lot already shines on the diamond
for baseball   the billboard on the corner

that changes once a month   moms & pops
are scared of tunnel we created as a makeshift
dugout hideaway too buried aliveness for them   glad

big supermarket comes to build   glad but sad
because the vacant lot got to go   Dickie say:
let's move all baseball to La Venezia Court: this

horseshoe deadend with famous Sunday funnies
clutter in the yards: Buck Rogers in the 25th
Century   Harold Teen {vestige of the past

tense even then}   Winnie Winkle the Bread
Winner   Dixie Dugan   Tillie The Toiler
Ella Cinders   the Heart of Juliet Jones

Brenda Starr {Girl Reporter}   they never did
flip for any liberation hyper-politics   never got
tense   they worked their woman thing   & went

to work with simple beauty in torn cartoon panel
fantasies   one time long after billboard baseball
vacant lot got bulldozed   robbers climb through

neighbor's window   knock over furniture   plenty
screams of stop dirty crooks stop stop   they escape
almost as though   they use tunnel

HOMILY FOR JEAN HARLOW

*The definition of beauty is easy;
it is what leads to desperation.*

— **Paul Valéry**

Kansas City born in 1911: uneducated at
Miss Barton's private school.
Parents divorced when she was 10.
Married at 16, in Lake Forest, to a man named
McGrew, moved to Los Angeles and became
Movie extra in Hal Roach comedy shorts.
Divorced, after she got top-billing in *Saturday Night Kid*.

Not so surprising her next film: is *Hell's Angels*
From Howard Hughes; where she's blasted by
Critics: however, they call her "star quality."
Then, her 1932 wedding with Irving Thalberg's
Right hand: Paul Bern who, after allegedly striking
Out at the matrimonial homeplate, took a pistol
And blended pieces of his brain with the wallpaper.

It was, also, speculated that he was murdered by
An irate relative of some tyrannical studio
Hotdog who, then, with elaborate precision and
Planning, planted evidence to make it look like
Suicide.

She flickered in *Red Dust, Hold Your Man* and
Bombshell; while a 1933 marriage to her
Cameraman was over by 1934.

Her film image begins to dim.

During the lensing of her 1937 resurgent movie
Saratoga, she does a LIFE magazine black/white
Photo shoot: Pacific Ocean: month of May: totally
Dressed-up; bone-white highheels putting divots
In the Malibu sand.

About four weeks subsequent to that, she snuffs
Behind complications from cerebral edema.

Her brain cells were white as beaches.

CHICAGO HOMILY
FOR KARYN KUPCINET

However as far as we're concerned, Karyn,
Concerning 1960s crossover beauties to
Television, your transformation turned you
Into feminine center for us all

However, being Kup's daughter: safe and
Secure in Chicago, but you made your
Beat out of town: only to end in an awful
Hollywood air-conditioned morgue on
Sweetzer: assailant unknown

However, we know the killer's name,
Don't we, Karyn? The one who stalks Death
Row Boulevard in Slaughter City, California!

However, just as Halstead Street is cause
Enough for Chicago blues: bad news on a
Daily Variety front cover causes us to cover
Our eyes, try to pray with this blue salute

However, Karyn, you who traveled West and
Traversed the terrain of despair, in a different
Way, remain a contemporary image of pretty
Girls who aren't so pretty, anymore

However, blocks beyond, now, we sneak like
Bandits down LaSalle Street: directly towards
The familiar deadend. We give our graveyard
Eyes a chance to glance up, as we do everyday,
And gaze at **The Goddess Of Grain**

GAIL RUSSELL

> *Ce reve ou l'amour consent*
> *a ouvrir son oeil encore un fois*
> —Artaud

without a doubt, our young & stricken hearts
in swirling muffy mist in 1943, were stranded
on a rooftop in Paris. here's the truth: we see
predictions of danky school girl kidnap & the
ransom of day-players who talk about your

cinematic soul. no: not the same way they move
in on tormented rhythm guitar picker chunk: or
wail-away rhythm & blues piano keyboard bomp,
but seeing you with our own eyes: your eyes
were ill filaments & seemed to crack open, as if

they were cast inside high-intensity lights. now,
while mad, sick, barbaric & dissolute audiences
watch you on television retrospect, you become some
supernatural observatory for the socially uninvited: or
they see you as an angel free from anthrax behind a

legend of cattle rustlers & through it all, they are unlike
loving fathers, but more like drunk uncles attending an
amazing May-day parade. this is the last audience who
can watch you the way they watched Carole Landis in
1940's myth, Gia Scala in the 1950's: the same way they

watched Jean Seberg shut-off by secret police in the
1960's: but never now even think about them for a minute
anymore. yes, they watch you, Gail, but barely look at your
eyes: broken headlights on a terrible taxi driving into a
country which grinds its gears & contemplates suicide.

A CONNECTICUT YANKEE IN THE KING ARTHUR MOTOR COURT JUST OUTSIDE LONG BEACH, CALIFORNIA

She's a niece of one of our teachers from fond
memory, yet snared in shadows of old gothic horrors

by immemorial former attractions to psycho-drama
novels like *King's Row*. But, all sentiments aside,

we seem to be escaping, now, down some royal shaft,
where a brood of holidays appears: familiar family

satellites represent a skulk of foxes with New England
falling away behind us: giving way to another time,

another dimension. Aeons dissipate like *Twilight Zone*
residuals. Today, we have taken our chariots as far as

Fountain Valley. We hold our camp outside Artesia
Meadows. Our tents are being pelted by a renegade

Wind. Any food which remains is tainted. In the morning
we will march towards the mountains, again.

MADONNA & PRINCE ARE INVITED ABOARD THE DEATHSTAR

After Jim Krusoe

At midnight Madonna & Prince climb aboard the
Deathstar. After they nosh on nacho cheese
Horsd'oeuvres, they are taken to their rooms
    which are decorated in the very latest
    Levitz furniture designs.
They have 4-wall video screens with constantly
    shifting images off MTV rotations from
    1986.
Prince gazes at the smash cuts of slam dance
    sequences & head banging thrasher music.
    He was secretly wishing they were slo-mo
    scenes of 1950's Main St. strippers wearing
    shoes with heels so high they had to pose
    leaning on bedposts or staircase railings.
Madonna worries one of her pink painted toenails
Into the ansanylon rug: she purrs into the intercom:
    "Wow, isn't this groovy, Prince?"
Prince replies: "If only Appollonia were here, it would
    all be so totally rad."
In actuality, Madonna & Prince haven't been so chilled &
At ease, since their game of *truth or dare* inside these new
Hypnotic environs: they no longer wanted to know
anything about what was going on outside: as a matter of
fact, if it's of any importance to anyone else down there
    in the real world, not a single citizen was aware of
    just exactly when the monsters had inhabited the
    city of Los Angeles. Or when blood began to bloom
    like puddles of spilled burgundy along Bundy Drive

ACT OF CONTRITION

I confess to the former Mafia casinos of Cuba that
Fidel Castro had a secret slot machine
And lost all his money

I confess to Che Guevara: betrayed like a
Columbian Dillinger, by the gun molls of
Guatemala

I confess to Allende, in Chile, murdered by
CIA terrorists; and Pablo Neruda's heart
Was broken forever

I confess to Mae Clarke that, if Cesar Chavez had
Been around, your face could have been spared any
Grapefruit humiliation; and the phrase "public enemy"
Would have suddenly taken on new meaning

I confess to Constance Moore that I've been
Backstage, with Jane Powell, holding a bouquet of
Roses, since 1945

I confess to Lana Turner: collapsing in a courtroom
In 1958; the heart of her gigolo paramour punctured
By a steak knife, in a bedroom, in Beverly Hills

I confess to Marilyn Monroe, in 1962 killed, according
To supermarket tabloids, by more murderers than any
Other victim in the history of the crime

I confess to John Belushi that speedballing cocaine was
Never ever tested as a salutary diet supplement

I confess to the U.S. Government who continues to
Blast billions of dollars worth of steel into space,
While Native Americans starve to death in
Wyoming

I confess to the raw sacrifice of 7 souls exploding
Into flaming coins of flesh over the
Florida coastline, as Capitalist politicians sit down
To 50-thousand-dollar-a-plate dinners in order to
Raise questions about the War On Poverty

I confess to Saint Bernadette who, in the form of
Jennifer Jones, married the Pasadena Art Museum
While we (children of the assassinated 1960s) tied-up
With construction paper, shooting nickel bags of
Elmer's Glue and, finally, OD'd on acrylic junk

I confess to Saint Therese for letting us hitch-hike to
Monaco and pray to our lady of yacht harbor,
Who happens to be a crypt-out hallucination of
Grace Kelly

I confess to All My Children: I confess to
The Young &The Restless: I confess to The Bold &
The Beautiful: I confess to The Days Of Our Lives:
 I confess to Another World, as well as to all other
Cancellations: I confess to the sacrament of
California, to God almighty, holy Christ: Forgive
America: forgive me for, like so many of the
Disenfranchised, I, too, am America

SILENCE IN A TALKING PICTURE
After the films of Dorothy McGuire

Et tacere est loqui cum Deo
— St. John of the Cross

As Claudia you burned the soup
and broke the Venetian blinds;
giving us enough time to cool off
between the wars, then unravel our

eyes to look through cleaner
windows. Somewhere, in back of
the black of memory reservoirs, we
are still waiting, as we might have

waited in 1952, for Louis Calhern's
invitation to a daughter saving you
from any past, lonely, funeral
impediment to your sweet speech. As

we continued to suffer inside our own
incurable diseases of disaffiliation,
we began to realize that no enchanted
cottage would ever inhabit our strained

sensibilities. Choosing to remain
sociopathic misfits, as a tree grows in
Brooklyn, we stay open to the weather
inside innocent human houses which,

sometimes, fail to surround us. We
approach the spiral staircase in our
mute American home, where mothers
and fathers remain emotionally disabled.

So much so that you are persuading us,
with gun-shy eyes, with amusement park
fascination for imperfection, with your
invalid mouth, finally, opening to scream;

allowing us to retreat into strange conformity
of the modern serial murder midnight re-run
television streets of our lives. Always where
grown-up relatives were telling us to be quiet.

A MAN MAD ENOUGH TO LIVE AMONG MONSTERS

I am a man mad enough to live among monsters,
Inside this blighted lightless place, where there are
Too many eyes, with nothing human looking out.

It's a place where a Dr. Frankenstein is seen lurking
Around every corner and waiting to create beasts of
 Dark malevolence; where weapons are sniping at

Innocent bystanders from turrets on tract-home
Prison rooftops. It is a place where there are too
Many being poisoned by the radiated grunge of

Industrial profiteering; or where they are terrorized
By landlords whose hands always get a firm grip on
Gears of the guillotine. Take me to a place, where

Jacaranda trees spill pills of purple cotton over
Pitted roads of passage; and, endlessly, leading
Back to that demonic country, where passports
Will always be issued for re-entry.

BIO-NOTE:

Michael C. Ford was born on the Illinois side of Lake Michigan. His debut LP vinyl which was a sequencing of air-checks from alternative radio appearances *(Language Commando)* earned a Grammy nomination in 1987. His volume of selected poems *(Emergency Exits)* was honored with a 1998 Pulitzer Prize nomination. His poem *Vietnam / Peace Casualties* was nominated for a 2006 Pushcart Prize. He's been invited to lecture at several universities, to be a frequent instructor for the Pen USA *Pen in the Classroom* program and to recite at various venues: many times with musical accompaniment.

www.ingramcontent.com/pod-product-compliance
Lightning Source LLC
Chambersburg PA
CBHW052029290426
44112CB00014B/2442